Once Lost Now Found

by Lauren English

Preface

Writing is an art. Growing up and going through high school I was continuously told by art teachers that art and creativity was not a talent that I possessed but little did I know then that literature was a form of art and it was one I had a strong passion for. I have always written for myself, to express my feelings and every dark emotion that has ever filled my being. It has always helped me; even reading back on poetry that I previously wrote, so now I pass it on, for others to try and find themselves in. This book contains all that I am and all that I have been. It's been carried around everyday in a pink notebook collecting memories of my good and bad days. It has been my guidance and now I hope it can be yours too. Whether or not I am a good writer is a different matter altogether, I write because I love to write, I'm not promising to be the next big thing...I'm just promising that what you are about to see is pure and genuine and true to me in every possible way.

Dedicated to the brightest lights of my life;

LP for getting me to where I am now

I am where I need to be

thank you

X

X

and

of course

the one who

stole my heart

and helped piece all

of my broken parts

back

together

X

X

my worlds

for keeping me strong

when I was weak

I love you all

X

desolated

desolated from existence

deprived of life

living in the darkness

and hiding from the light

-my mental state

who will be there when I need them?

who will pick me up when I'm down?

who will get me through the day?

that's right; no one

-I am   alone

skipping one meal won't hurt

or two

maybe even three

I'll only lose weight, right?

-wrong. how could I be so stupid

I'm not living; I'm surviving

taking it one day at a time

trying not to fall off the edge

-tomorrow is a new day

if you knew that I'm still hurting

would you care?

would you feel guilty?

when you hear my name

what do you remember

the good or the bad

or nothing

-I loved you and you broke me

you'll be okay

one day

It's not the end

so just hold on

-you've got this

a thousand fragments

shattered into insignificant parts

helpless and broken

in need of repair

longing for a miracle

but I seen one no where

then from out of the blue

my miracle had risen

and I escaped from my mortal prison

-you stole the keys and set me free

I'm scared.

scared of losing you

and scared of being alone

if I lost you

I would lose myself

and I can't handle that

-please don't leave me

my heart speeds up

I panic

and I drop

-anxiety at its finest

I could have been anything

I could have set my dreams high

and broke my walls down

but instead I panicked

-now I'm ordinary

when you're incapable of raising your hand

speaking out loud

asking for help

walking past groups of people

that's when you know there is a problem

-I'm riddled with social anxiety

the heart doesn't break

it is pulverized into meaningless

pieces that will never be whole again

-you ruined me

you told me that you loved me

I truly thought that you cared

I should have known

I should have known better than to believe in you

you broke me;

sinking my heart

until it was nothing more than a ship wreck

lying in the pit of my stomach

crumbling and decaying

over time with all the life drained

I was emptied

-how do you recover

the sound of silence

can sometimes be the

l o u d e s t

although you may be

alone your inner demons

scream louder than ever

-when will the noise stop

no parent should lose their child

no parent should have to hold their baby's

lifeless body in their frail arms

no parent should go through that pain

watching the men in black carry the pure white coffin

knowing what lies beneath the flower coated lid.

hearing screams of pain

as their angel gets laid to rest

whilst they say their last goodbye

-but it will never really be the last

as my chest tightens

I can feel my surroundings slip away

everything begins to go blank

as nothing but white noise fills my ears

my head spins

my legs will give up soon

but then I remember your words

I am where I need to be

and all I have to do is breath

-lana parrilla fixed me

let go. I'm ready.

ready to soar into the great beyond

ready to spread my wings and fly

fly higher than any mountain, bird or plane

I'm free.

but then something occurs to me

I'm leaving the ones I love

the ones who love me

I see your small angelic face

from the world above

I can't leave you, so I pull myself back

letting you hold onto the shiny inflatable

for a few more seconds

the words "I miss you" spread across the front

I'll miss you too but it's time

time to go now

goodbye sister, I'll see you again

one day

hopefully not too soon

-balloons hold so much symbolism

you never take the quote

you don't know what you've got until its gone

too seriously until all you had is gone

you can be angry

upset

you can hate the world;

and everyone in it

but one day you will pick up your broken pieces

and single handily put them back together

be fearless

be brave

-you will be okay

maybe I care too much

it's a good thing

yet also a bad

a strength

and a weakness

but I can't exactly stop caring

-I can't do that right?

you walk in and I'm a tomato

and I am ready to be

squashed

-h e l p

you were my favourite kind of drug

causing happiness and taking away the pain

making me feel good

really good

but little did I know

you were demolishing me one day at a time

-drugs are illegal for a reason

you wanted me to be extraordinary

but that's not something I could be

instead I'm plain and simple

and that's something known as

being me

-I am who I am

I hope that one day

you look back

and realise

that you let go of a rare diamond

to go and play with the pebbles

-I'm not easy to forget

if I could be strong all the time

I would be

but I can't

so, don't expect me too

-I'm a work in progress

look at me through my eyes

and tell me what you see

you might then understand

just how much I hate

me.

-forever a train wreck

we have been torn at the seams

and everyday

we are getting worn down

until we are nothing but

an unravelled romance

-no tailor can fix this

if you can't see the good

in yourself

how is anyone else

supposed too

-believe in yourself

I didn't think it was capable of happening

until it happened.

I broke

I was ruined

intentionally or not

you broke me

-never ask for my forgiveness

you were the snow

that cascaded my heart

making me feel pretty for a while

before freezing

stone cold black ice

and becoming everyone's

worst nightmare

-eternally grateful that you melted away

little did I know

that the one who

who would soothe my pain

at 3am

would be the main cause of my tears

at 3am

-I guess you were too good to be true

when a child's toy breaks

you throw it away

but what do you do

if the thing that breaks

is your heart

-broken beyond repair

losing you felt like

having water slowly

but surely fill my lungs

becoming short of breath

until finally I was nothing

but the remains

of the girl you ruined

-I drowned in my emotions

our love felt like a carousel

constantly revolving

we would break up

then make up

and it wouldn't stop

-I had to get off that ride

the word fat

seared into my mind

onto my skin

and forever in my heart

-words hurt

I'm lost

and I need to be found

so please

come and find me

-I'm desperate

tears spilled from

her crystalized eyes

he was gone

and she knew

that he wasn't coming back

-he promised to never leave and he did

in my head

there is always yelling

even when there's no sound

my demons work together;

they are the best team around

but their one goal in life

is to bring me down

-and they are winning

I'm falling.

my legs have numbed

I can't get up

I feel trapped

I don't know what to do

what can I do?

-nothing. I do nothing

a tsunami tumbled down

wiping out her fragmented heart

and discolouring her soul until

it was jet black and hollow

they damaged me

she whispered

-but no one was there to reply

her memory remains suppressed

as everyone forgets the child

that once was.

obliterated and erased

from their history

like it never even happened

-I won't forget you

all the people I know

are New York, London, Tokyo

and then there is me

small, unknown

but concealing dreams

that are too big for this

small town

-if only

if we aren't honest

then are we

worth anything anymore?

-its killing me

this world could corrupt

the kindest of souls

exploiting others and

mistreating people

is foreseen as okay

this is a world where

the sinners are seen

as the saints

-do people still have morals

I was an explosive

in the hands of

an open flame

once you set me off

we were burning to the ground

-no turning back

my words grew thick

suddenly they didn't just

pour from my mouth

my ability to speak

was cut

-ability to speak to you anyway

you were my

greatest urgency

but I was only your

occasional craving

-and no one likes cravings

when you left I felt

paralysed

I wanted to move forward

but I couldn't

-your love disabled me

I loved dolls

I loved being in control

making them do what

I wanted them to do

but I never thought

that one day

someone would find

the power to make me

their doll

-manipulated

it still hurts

and I'm still sad

but you're out of my life

and for that

I'm glad

-goodbye

you were that

"one too many" shot of tequila

great at the time

yet deadly the next day

-I was never a big drinker anyway

are you okay?

yes.

she lied

are you sure?

of course.

again, she lied

-how could she tell the truth

a bullet shot through

my chest

would hurt less

than watching you

walk out of my life

-you may as well pull the trigger

things you said you wouldn't do;

hurt me

leave me

break me

forget me

things you did;

-all the above

you were the ethereal
aspect of my life
whilst I was a
hellish wrath
upon you
-I was Satan. You were the angel

my heart was bound to you

like an ancient book

that had been boxed for years

-not very well

beckoning you here

was easy

making you stay

was hard

-thanks for leaving

the weight

shed from my bones

until I was nothing but

a risk of snapping

-skin and bone and still not skinny enough

her walls were

built up so high

but she came

along and knocked them down

like a standing trail of dominoes

-my love won my heart

and it hurts to know

that you are happy with

someone new.

not because I'm jealous

but because of the pain

you put me through

-you don't deserve happiness

at night I allow

rivers to pour from my eyes

and a stream of

emotion to flow from

my heart

it morphs itself

into words which

I then print in

my messy scrawl

onto paper

and pass it off as art

-poet at work

she sits alone

waiting.

hoping.

even praying that someone

will catch a glimpse of her,

see her red puffy eyes

which has tear stained cheeks to match

that someone will notice the

outline of the bandage

that wraps around her battle wounds

that you can see ever so slightly

through her long-sleeved shirt

wishing that just one person

will see that

she is fading away

beneath her baggy clothing

she is nothing but skin and bone

she's screaming louder than ever

on the inside

but on the outside

s i l e n c e

-mental illness

if there was another

would you let me go?

If I was just an option

would our love still flow?

I wonder if you would care

I wonder

-I really wonder

once made of stone

now falling apart

-like an old building

turned to ice

frozen from the inside out

I patiently wait to thaw

but I have no luck

for you always remain

cold hearted

-your presence chills me

lost and insecure

but who really

found me

-let's find out

vigorously crying

into the bedsheets

night after night

patiently waiting;

waiting and hoping

that someday

I'll get through this

-lying to myself

the darkness lingers over me

and I push it aside

but one day

I'll give in

and let it

consume me

-death

you're right there

yet I feel more alone than ever

do you even notice me?

have I even caught your eye?

this is meant to be a game played by two

yet I've took the wheel and

I'm doing this singlehandedly

-this game sucks

we are like x's and o's

I'm constantly going in circles

to try and make you happy

and you are crossing me out

like I'm nothing

-it's just a game to you

two grieving mothers;

one young, one old

one muffled and one bold

one had fifty years

one had ten

but never the less

they are still mothers

who lost their child

far too soon

-goodbye angel

it's strange how

a life of a loved one

can be remembered

in under an hour

within that time

they have been

spoke about

sang about

cried over

and put in the ground

to never be seen again

-but they will be remembered

that wound has closed

I've had time to heal

that chapter has ended

and I've started again

but from time to time

there is a surge of pain

and it's like that old scar

has been torn open again

-I wish this was about a real wound

intoxication breaks you down

rips you apart limb by limb

it's an addiction

a killer

-and so were you

just because I've been

getting better it doesn't mean

that I am better

-gradual process

you are selfish

and you hurt me

all the time

you don't care about me

or anything I do

you hurt me

-you continuously hurt me

are you ready?

no, I'll never be ready

I'll never be ready to say goodbye,

to let go

-it's not as easy as it looks

I was fine

until I wasn't

it was an abrupt change

going from happiness

to pure devastation

-I broke

flashlights

your eyes take me to a new world

I am mesmerised and captivated

your beauty is astonishing

it will forever blow my mind

-I'm crazy about you

a fantasy world of mythical creatures

every page is a new adventure

and every book is a new life

-literature saved me

having passion is a gift;

it's a desire to make a difference

and seeing the best in the darkest of times

it's spreading positivity

and radiating light

-be a Streep in a world full of Kardashians

I close my eyes and see you

it's always you

no one else

just you

-you're my one and only

you make me really giggly

like a kid with a crush

giving me butterflies with every glance

and making me believe in our hopeless romance

-mine

a home isn't a home;

it isn't four walls, some windows and a door

it's you.

an out of rhythm heart beat

with a beautiful smile

and arms that I longed to be in for a while

it's acceptance and love

and never being forgotten

-home is with you

I miss you

today, tomorrow, and forever

I miss you

-why are you so far away

being in love

its seeing things from a different perspective

not only do you think of what you want

but what you both want

it's looking at that special someone

and knowing that you wouldn't want to be with another

its accepting that they are not perfect

that no one is

but loving them endlessly

it's not being afraid to fall

because you know they will catch you

its putting yourself;

your faith and your trust

into them without having doubts

-I'm committed to you

you're my person

my best friend

you're the reason

for my daily smile

-friendship is everything

I guess I'm just

in love

-we are a fairy-tale

I don't need a red leather jacket

a wand

a shield

a suit made of steel

I need my girls

-they are my armour

happiness is hearing your voice

and seeing your face

its knowing that in a matter of days

we will be together again

-long distance isn't easy

our love is red

romantic and warm

with a tendency to burn

-it's sad but it's true

vulnerability in the hands

of the right person

is a gift

-you make everything okay

you made every day feel like a dream

but I am awake

and this isn't a dream

-it's very real

Romeo

was never afraid of loving

Juliet

so why am I afraid

of loving you?

-every love story has its doubts

shaking

trembling in fact

years of waiting

came down to this moment

and then you appear

in front of me

and before I know it

tears escape from my eyes

and I know

that for the first time

I am where I am meant to be

-29/4/17

through storms I would go

breaking down mountains

on my way

walking, climbing, surviving

all to see your face

-240 miles means nothing

365 days

12 months

4 seasons

52 weeks

and I spend them

being in love with you

-we are a repeated annual kind of love

I try to say it

I really do

but my words,

they won't come out right

but I love you

I really do

-never forget

it's a long winding road

and I'm nowhere near the end

but with the right people

this treacherous walk

is more of a casual stroll

-life is easier with friends

is love enough?

enough to keep me sane

to keep me holding on

love may not be enough

but you

you are enough

-always

your name melts like butter

soft and gentle

it is the sweetest sound

there's nothing I love more

-I could spend my life saying your name

with one click of a button

I found you

imagine how different

things would be

if I didn't press that button

-I wouldn't be here

I'm seeking for answers

but I'm only finding them

in your eyes

-your eyes show more emotion than your words

I cherish your

every word

every breath

every breath

every move

they complete me

-you complete me

I was a flight risk

and you ripped

off my wings

so I wouldn't fly away

again

-not that I was going too

wrap your arms around me

just one more time

please

let me feel at home again

one last time

-her arms felt like coming home

you are everything to me

but to you

I'm just another fan

-and I'm proud to be just that

that same calendar

yet the date stays the same

and why they ask

because I'm not ready

to stop living out my dream

-dreams do come true

"you'll never meet your idol"

they said

"she won't be as nice in person"

they said

and they were wrong

I met her

and she was more amazing

than I ever imagined

-she was indescribable

she has a beautiful face

with distinct solemn features

that had changed over the years

never the less she still had no

imperfections

her smile is warming

and it fills their beings with love

-a one of a kind mother

you raised me to be truthful

to be caring and to be kind

you made me strong with

every word

and you would never of

left me behind

from the day of my first steps

I've walked carefully by your side

because I know that

you will pick me up when I fall

-dad

curves on any girl

are beautiful

-especially her smile

it's all fiction to you

but to me it's everything

every character

every season

every plot twist

its everything

it has shaped me

and because of this fiction

I am the person that I am

-it's not just a show

you paint rainbows

into my dull skies

you give the lyrics

to every song

a meaning

you give my existence

a purpose

-my saviour

the stars seem closer

when your around

the impossible

is made to be possible

when your around

I can do anything

if you're around

-please stay around

backwards

forwards

and it doesn't stop

it's a constant movement

and it doesn't stop

-this is repetitive like the movement of this ship

your love was the CPR

that I needed

to bring me back

after having my aorta rupture

and almost

bleeding out on the table

-near death experience

our memories have been

scorched into my mind

and carefully chiselled

onto my heart

-you are my forever

missing you is

a chronic illness

on the heart

its manageable for a while

but one day it will wipe me

clean out

-I wish I didn't miss you so much

our hands interlock

like two weaving branches

that manage to grow;

starting off apart

and slowly but surely

coming together

-we are one

I see you floating around

gracefully like a feather that is

caught in the midst of a gale

your being is filled with

so much serenity

-you stole my heart

you are my angel in disguise

protecting me from the dark

and re-introducing me to the light

-personal guardian

a baby's

laughter is the

most precious sound

treasure it

-it won't last forever

and in that moment, I remembered

where my hands really belonged

it was as clear as a summer sky

they should be linked with yours

by our sides

in a place we call our own

-we belong together

looking into her eyes

for the first time

felt like going home

being in her arms

for the first time

was safety in its own

beautiful way

meeting my idol

for the first time

completed me

-its where I was meant to be

—

If you have made it this far then I applaud you just as I applaud myself. You have just walked with me hand in hand through the darkest times of my life, to finding my very own flashlights that have guided me through to where I am now; the self-love stage. I am slowly learning to love myself for who I am and the person that I have become. It has been a long journey and with the help of my guardian angels I am sure that one day I will pull myself out the other side, put on a permanent smile and shout "I made it" to everyone who told me that I wouldn't. Always remember that tough times don't last forever but tough people most certainly do.

—

recovering

I'm not afraid of the unknown

what happens will happen

I can't hide from the inevitable

not anymore anyway

-face your fears

I am a warrior

my armour keeps me steady

your heart keeps me strong

I am unbreakable

-you will never tear me down

the scales don't define me

it's a pointless number

that can no longer have power,

can no longer hold me prisoner

now I'm breaking my shackles

and setting myself free

anorexia doesn't make me who I am

I make me who I am

-I saved myself

if we were both stars

you'd swear that you shine brightest

and that's what proves

that I am in fact

the brighter star

-life isn't a competition

I built my own castle

and made myself the queen

I became the unstoppable

and now I conquer over all

-take control of your life

society is changing

but I'm not

when children plaster their faces

and terror is caused in the streets

everything is changing

everyone I know has changed

but me

I stay the same

-don't change too fit in

why be scared of tomorrow

if you refuse to deal with today

who knows what the future will bring

it's a mystery to us all

that will only be revealed

with time

-take a chance

eat something

ignore the calories

they don't matter

you are what matters

-you don't need to break yourself to make yourself

be a hurricane

an uncontrollable force of nature

take control

and hold the power

-you are capable of so much

I want to be a child again

so I can run free

I'd be carefree

nothing would matter

-let's rewind the clock

the words I do

tying two souls together

for all of time

a permanent bond and a promise;

a promise for eternal love

through the good and bad

no matter what

-but in the end, they are only words

your fairy tales are straight and narrow

but mine enhanced my life

I fell in love

character by character

and before I had time to realise

my life revolved around

Once Upon A Time

-it is everything to me

I'm not a weekend get away

I'm a permanent stay

-don't come calling when it suits you

your body is your own

blank canvas

paint it in the way

you would like too

and don't let anyone tell you

to stop

-embrace the artist inside of you

I'm living

in a world where

girls kissing girls

is seen as a sin

yet men that

are assaulting women

is seen as okay

-what has the world came too

I'm a girl

and I kiss girl(s)

is that a problem?

if so you know

where the exit is

-National Coming Out Day

we grow

and age

and live out our life

only too fade away

into oblivion

-create your legacy and be remembered

I was the

incongruous soul

in a world full of

congruous beings

I was never one

too fit in

and I mingled in the crowds

and I was okay with that

-lone ranger

bravery swept a

nation of people away

as she woke up from

the mass spell of insecurity

that controlled her being

today I will be free

-I will be me

I forgive you

in spite of everything

you have done

not because I think

that what you did is okay

but because

I'm not as shallow

as you are

-you are forgiven

breath in;

think of the positives

and all of the good in your life

breath out

and accept that if

you are capable of

functioning a heart

then you are capable

of so much more

-opportunities are your oxygen; it keeps you breathing

don't throw away

something you spent

a lifetime searching for

because even if they come back

it will never really

be the same again

-keep holding on

the food you consume

is not the villain

in your fairy tale

the villain is todays

generation trying to

define perfection

-you aren't your disorder

I'll spend my life fighting

fighting for what I believe in

at least then if I don't succeed

I will die saying I tried

-equal rights is an ongoing battle

believe in yourself

even if you feel like

no one else is there

cheering you on

just lift your head up high

and be your own

applauding audience

-self belief is a wonderful thing

if I lost my life tomorrow at least

I could say that I've lived

I've loved

I've lost

I've gained strength

and found my weaknesses

I've moved mountains

to find my happiness

and I found it

-I never thought I'd find it

Printed in Great Britain
by Amazon

74298899R00090